STEVE BAIL
VICTOR WOOTEN
BASS
EXTREMES

Editor: Aaron Stang
Assistant Editor: Albert Nigro
Transcriptions by: Roy Vogt
Photography: Margaret Ford
Cover Design: Debbie Johns Lipton
Cover Background Image: © Photo Disk, Inc.

Special Guest: Gregg Bissonette on Drums
Produced by: Steve Bailey and Victor Wooten
Recorded at: Slam Shack, N. Hollywood, CA
Mixed by: Steve Bailey,
      Victor Wooten and
      Brian Springer

Copyright © 1993 Beam Me Up Music, c/o CPP/Belwin, Inc.
15800 N.W. 48th Avenue, Miami, FL 33014

International Copyright Secured   Made in U.S.A.   All Rights Reserved

MW01487133

Special Thanks From Steve To:

...Allan and everyone at Aria U.S.A.; David and Chris at ADA
...Mark and Hector at JBL
...Pat, Becky and everyone at B.I.T.
...Steve Reid and Gregg Bissonette, for being a <u>monster</u>!
...Jim, Chris, Scott and Karl at Bass Player Magazine.
...Margaret Ford, The Best.
...Bass Magazine, Japan; All the Bassists and Musicians who inspired this work.
...Aaron Stang and Sandy Fieldstein at CPP/Media for making this happen.
...Eichi and Penny at Domo Music Group; and Mom and Dad.
...My Bass Brother Victor for being Victor!

Special Thanks From Victor To:

...Holly Goldman;
...Mom, Dad, Regi, Roy, Rudy and Joseph Wooten;
...Steve Bailey, for coming up with the idea, for playing so great and for being such a great
   friend (also for being short, like me);
...Greg Bissonette, for playing incredibly well and for seeing that 3D art so fast;
...Stanley Clarke, Jaco Pastorious, Chick Corea, and many other for being such a big part of
   this project;
...Aaron Stang and all the people at CPP/Belwin;
...Jenny Hoeft, for adding spice to the session, John Billings for coming by and teaching me
    some new licks;
...Fodera Guitars, ADA, and D'Addario Strings.

Thanks to all of you for listening.
  Peace;
  Vic

Contents

	Contents	CD Program Log

About The Book

Steve Bailey and Victor Wooten have put together this incredible bass showcase. These recordings emphasize the tremendous, often unrealized, potential of the bass as both a lead and accompanying instrument. On the recording, Steve and Victor demonstrate how the bass can supply bass lines, piano and guitar type comping figures, lead solos and percussion, in styles ranging from Bebop to New Age to Heavy Metal - all without overdubs. Each piece highlights different aspects of their amazing techniques; like Steve's three finger technique and his awe inspiring command of harmonics and chord voicings; or Victor's incredible funk grooves, thumb and two handed tapping techniques. Because of their incredible ability to simultaneously play bass lines and chords it often sounds as if each part is actually played by two bass players. At the end of the song section of the recording, Steve and Victor walk you note-for-note through the licks and techniques that make up each tune, explaining and demonstrating everything at slow speeds. Victor is panned a little to the right and Steve a little to the left.

The book explains all of the techniques and licks used in each song. Both bass parts are fully transcribed in notation and tablature.

A Chick From Corea

In this first piece, Victor is playing the tenor bass (A-D-G-C tuning) and Steve is playing a fretless 6 string (B-E-A-D-G-C tuning). While Victor takes the melody in the A section, Steve uses his thumb, index, ring and middle fingers to create a chordal accompaniment (see Example 1).

Even if you play a four-string bass you can still use this technique. Try the voicings in Example 2A. After you have them under control, try moving the entire ii-V-I cadence by whole-steps: Dm7-G7-C, Cm7-F7-Bb, Bbm7-Eb7-Ab, etc. When you can do this smoothly, try adding the artificial harmonics found in Example 3A. Playing the chord in harmonics will make the chord voicings stand out more clearly.

Victor's single line playing really shines on this tune. Try the "chicken pickin'" in Example 4 and the melody in Example 5. Start slowly and gradually increase the tempo, using a drum machine or metronome for reference. Since this is all played on a tenor bass, you might try taking this down an octave or even restringing a spare bass in tenor tuning. You can even take a spare 5-string and tune it E-A-D-G-C a la Steve Swallow!

Example 1

In this song, Steve takes a supportive role playing chords and bass lines. The bass line to the A section is:

Example 2

Here, Steve demonstrates both styles of music – *Country & Western* – with a very guitaristic "boom chick" part. The root and 5th are played on the two low strings and the 7th and 3rd of the chord are played on the 3rd and 4th strings.

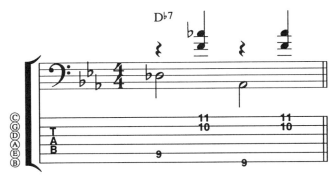

Example 2A shows how the same type of pattern can be applied to a 4-string bass.

Example 2A

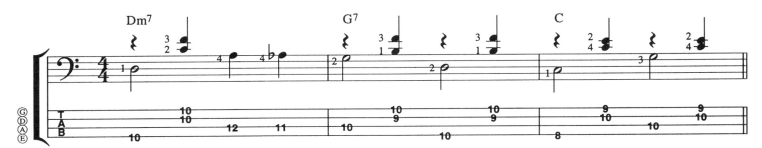

Example 3

Harmonics can be added by touching the string one octave (12 frets) above the fretted note with the index finger and plucking the string with the ring finger, all while playing the alternating bass line.

Note: A detailed description of artificial harmonic technique is found in Steve's *Advanced Rock Bass,* available from CPP/Belwin.

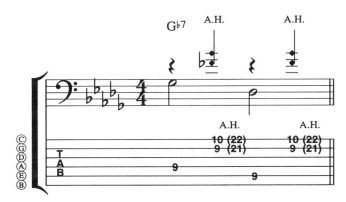

Example 3A

Here is a 4-string fingering for this harmonic technique.

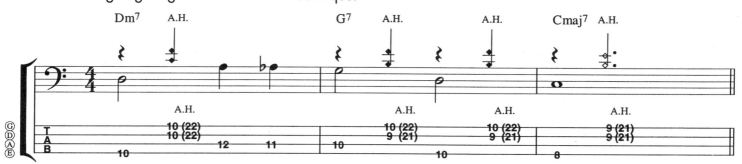

Example 4

On this song, Victor played the tenor bass which is tuned: A-D-G-C (up a 4th from the regular four-string bass). He plucked the strings harder than usual to get that "chicken picking" guitar sound. To get this effect, hook your fingers under the strings and "snap" each note. You can also create this effect by simply picking harder, using conventional right hand technique:

Example 5

Here, Victor demonstrates, at a slow tempo, the melody from "A Chick From Corea."

Bangkok Blues

Bangkok Blues is a great example of how two different players can approach the same concept. This tune is primarily a feature for Steve, and it shows how he can use artificial harmonics in conjunction with fretted notes to create a three octave spread in the double-stopped melody (Example 6). In addition, pay attention to the "impossible" chord voicings in the B section. Steve is using the string bass concept of the "thumb position" to hold the F pedal point with his thumb. This allows a greater reach for chords and enables the bassist to add upper extensions (9ths and 13ths) to the chord voicings.

Victor produces widely spread voicings by using a two-handed tapping technique (Example 7). You can get your bearings on this technique by taking something as simple as a C scale and playing it with two hands (Example 7A). Just remember to anchor the right hand thumb on the top of the neck when you're tapping. This gives you more power and a better articulation.

Example 6

In this song the melody is played in "double octaves." For example: D is played in octaves with the lower note on the E string and the upper note on the C string; then Steve uses his right hand index and ring fingers to play the harmonic 12 frets above the upper D.

And the same with the melody:

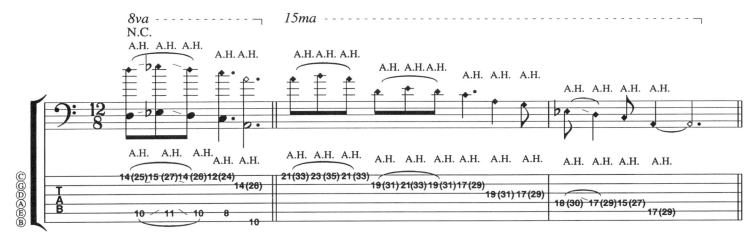

Example 7

Victor uses a two-hand tapping technique to achieve the same two octave spread as in Example 1. He taps the lower D on the A string (5th fret) with his left hand and with his right hand he taps the high D on the G string (19th fret). Victor adds vibrato to the long tones to give them a more vocal quality.

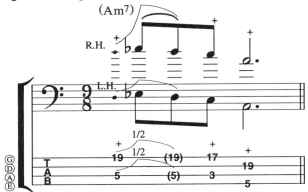

The two-handed technique that Victor is using utilizes both hands, each tapping the same notes, octaves apart. Try this with the following C scale. (Example 7A). Note that the right and left hand fingerings are identical.

Example 7A

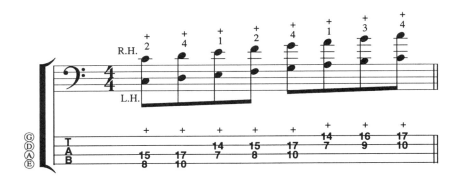

To help get a better right-hand attack, anchor the right-hand thumb on the top of the neck. This next exercise is played right-hand only.

Example 7B

Stan the Man

Victor is back on tenor bass as he and Steve pay tribute to legendary bassist Stanley Clarke. The melody is supported by a strong modally-based chord progression. This is a Clarke trademark, as are the open string chords Steve solos over.

Example 8 shows how Steve uses artificial harmonics in conjunction with fretted notes to outline the chords (E/G♯, A, E/B, & C♯m), Check out the recording to hear him do this, while really locking in and grooving with Greg Bissonette.

Steve demonstrates his three finger technique for high speed runs in Example 9. You could call it "3 x 3" because he plays 3 notes per string with 3 right-hand fingers (i m a). He explains both of these concepts in full in his book: *Rock Bass.*

Victor uses a radically different approach for his high speed work. Using his thumb like a guitar pick he "double thumbs" using down and up strokes of the thumb, and then adds an index finger "pop" to play incredibly fast triplets (see Example 10A). After you've got the basic technique down, try 3 notes (10B) and then 3 notes per string (10C).

Example 8

Here, Steve combines a bass line with chords voiced above. Steve plays the chord tones arpeggio style, in harmonics.

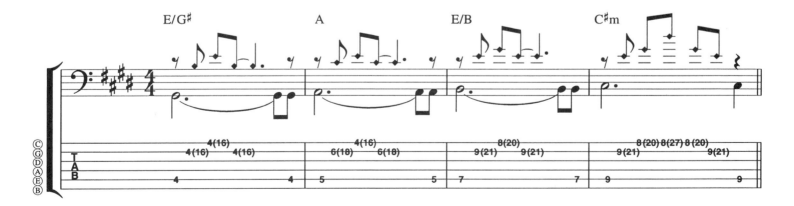

Example 9

Steve has an interesting technique for producing the fast triplet passages found in the solo section of this song; this technique involves a three finger right hand technique. Usually the fingering is "a m i" with all three notes played on one string.

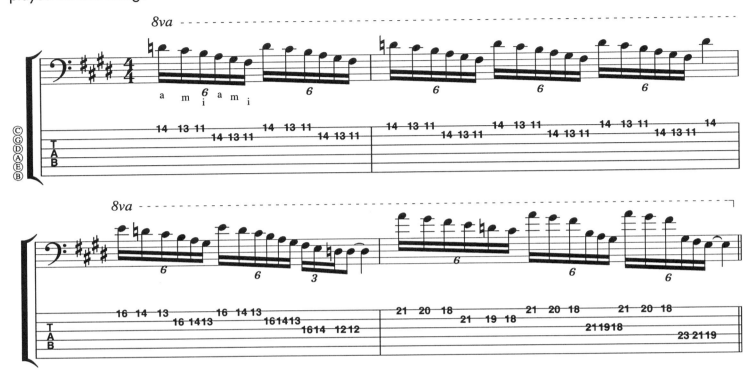

Example 10

Having been very influenced by Stanley Clarke, Victor sought ways to emulate his speed and technique. He found that by using his fingers alone he was unable to play triplet passages as fast as Stanley and so developed an interesting technique involving the right hand thumb and index finger. He uses a down-up stroke of the thumb followed by the index finger to produce the three separate attacks.

Example 10A (one note triplet exercise):

Example 10B (three notes):

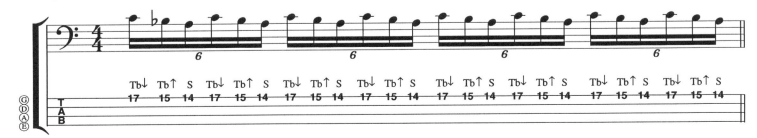

Example 10C (six notes):

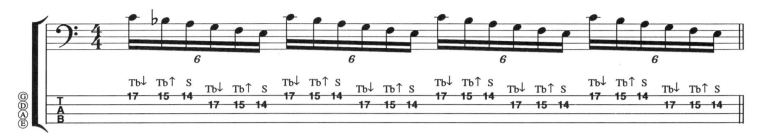

Example 11

In order to further emulate the Stanley Clarke sound, Victor uses a tenor bass (tuned: A-D-G-C) with a lot of high end and a very sharp attack.

On this song, Victor uses mainly the E major pentatonic scale (shown here fingered for a standard four-string bass):

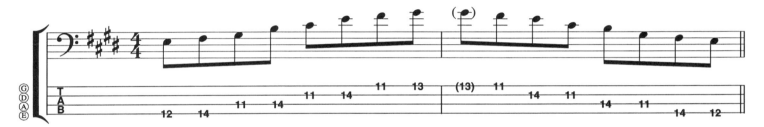

You can hear from the example on the recording, that the scale works well for all of the chords.

Victor's Jam

Victor's Jam showcases Victor's jaw-dropping slap technique. If you've been fortunate enough to see him live or on video, you've probably noticed how little movement he requires to create a flurry of notes. This is due to his use of both hands together. You can get your feet wet with the "open hammer pluck" technique shown in Example 12. Then, add more notes by using index and middle finger pops. This is done in one rolling motion with the right hand and creates a "flam," like a drummer plays (Example 13). After you get this down try Example 14 and then the entire solo. Just remember to start slowly, use a metronome to stay steady, and be very patient.

Example 12: The Open Hammer Pluck

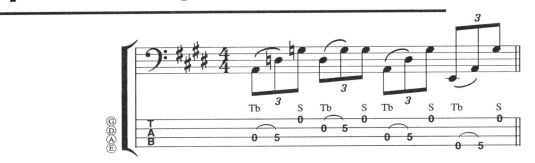

Example 13

Most bass players will use a down stroke of the thumb, followed by an upward pluck with the index finger. If you combine the thumb with an upward pluck of both the index and middle finger you can get a very fast triplet, which, when muted, gives an effect similar to a drummers flam.

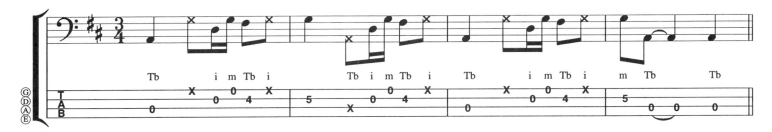

You can also apply notes to this technique and produce fast scale and arpeggio techniques. It's easier than it sounds, so experiment with the technique and have some fun; just make sure you groove with the drummer!

Example 14

Here is an example of the main bass riff upon which this tune is built. Note the use of the open string "hammer pluck" technique.

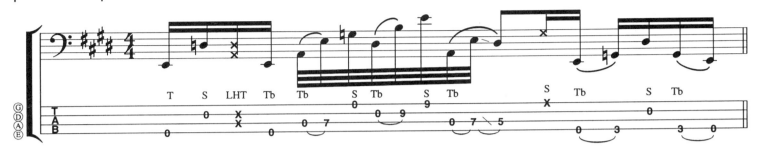

Thumb Start My Harley

This tune continues to showcase Victor's funk prowess. Example 15 shows a more advanced "open hammer pluck" pattern that relies on rapid string crossing for its impact. It really sounds a lot harder than it is, so give it a shot. When you can play the sextuplets smoothly try the basic groove pattern found in Example 15A.

Steve gets to really cut loose on the opening cadenza! He's using a combination of delay, distortion, compression and reverb to create his sound. The fretless really becomes one huge whammy bar. In this case, the sound really helps to give the notes more impact. So break out your effects and go to town.

Example 15

Here is yet another example of Victor's spectacular triplet technique. As you can see, once you have a command of these basic techniques, they can be applied in many different ways to many styles and playing situations.

This example utilizes the "open hammer pluck" technique (see Example 12). Here, Victor begins by playing an open A, followed by a "hammer" at the octave on that string (A, 12th fret). Then "pluck" the open G with the right hand index finger; this produces the first triplet. The second half of this lick uses the same techniques. Play the open D, then "hammer" the E at the 14th fret on the same string. Now "pluck" a high B on the G string (16th fret). Now slide the lick down a whole step (use the same open strings).

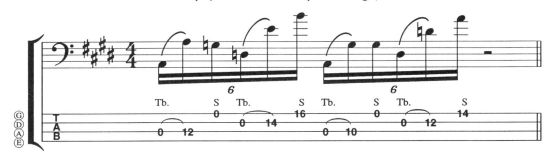

Example 15A

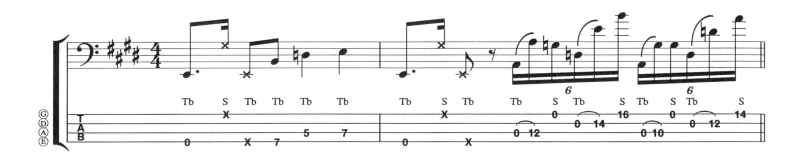

Example 16

In this song, Steve essentially plays a "lead guitar" part, using a *Korg A1* for distortion. Using the stereo outs on the unit, he then blended his dry (no effect) and wet sounds (with effects) in the mix. Along with distortion, Steve is also using an aural exciter (to add presence), compression and delay.

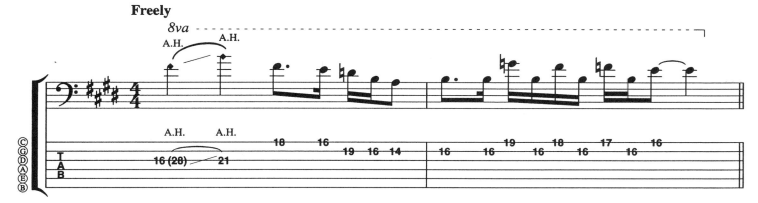

Example 17

Both artificial and natural harmonics are used to get the really high notes, further giving the impression of a lead guitar, rather than a bass.

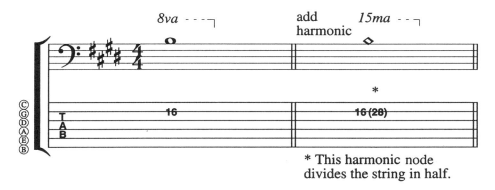

* This harmonic node
divides the string in half.

Example 18

The sound of a Harley revving up is produced by sliding up the fingerboard on the fretless bass.

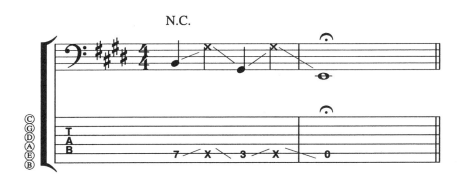

Emerald Forest

Emerald Forest showcases Victor's two-handed accompaniment and Steve's fluid fretless work. By playing two notes with each hand, Victor creates a rolling bed of 6th chords for Steve to solo over (Example 19). Using the ii-V-I cadence from Example 2, you can create the same kind of rolling effect (Example 19A). Like the previous pattern, try moving it around in whole steps.

Steve uses a different approach to this same effect in Example 20. He creates a rolling arpeggio with artificial harmonics and moves to the upper node 17 frets above the fretted note. This produces a note one octave and a fifth above the fundamental and adds upper extensions to the chord voicings (see *Advanced Rock Bass*).

Example 19

On this song, Victor lays down a two-handed tapping ostinato bass part providing a pad, over which Steve can play the melody and improvise. The first half of the ostinato pattern is derived from an E major pentatonic scale beginning on low E on the E string. The pattern then repeats, up a fourth from A on the A string. In the following examples the notes played by the left hand are stems down and the notes played by the right hand are stems up.

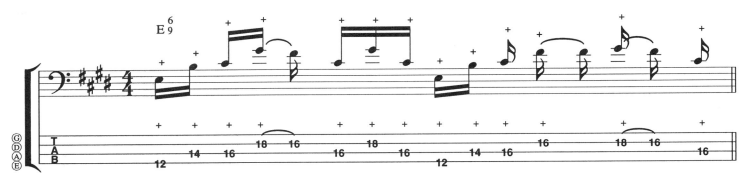

Example 19A: (not on recording)

A ii-V-I cadence using two-handed tapping technique.

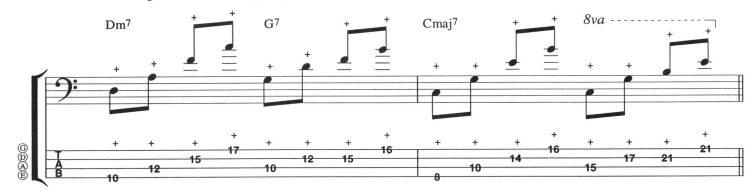

Example 20

Here, Steve sounds like two people playing at once. He plays a bass line while simultaneously playing an arpeggio-style accompaniment part in harmonics.

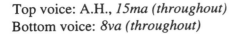

Top voice: A.H., *15ma (throughout)*
Bottom voice: *8va (throughout)*

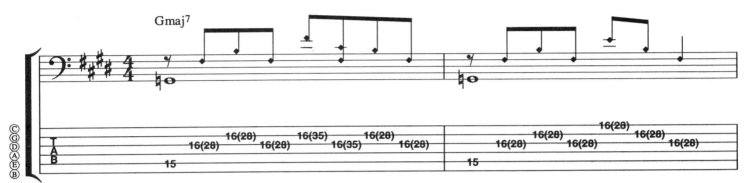

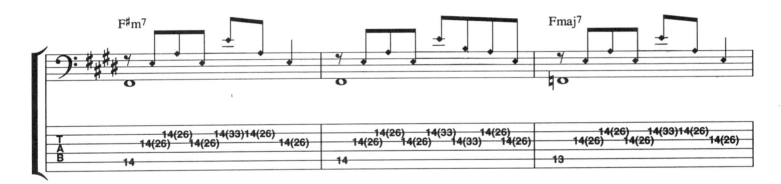

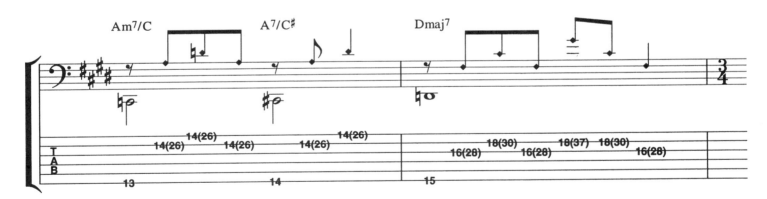

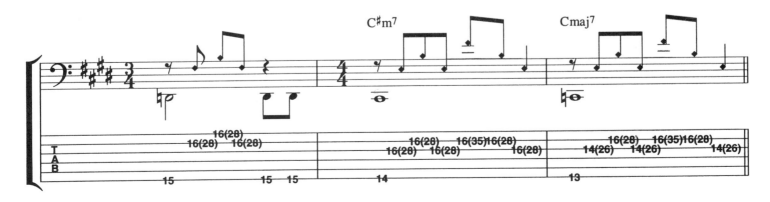

Moonridge

This is Steve's solo piece. In it, he relies on an open D drone string to serve as a pedal for the moving voices in the chords (Example 21). Note Steve's signature use of artificial harmonics. In Example 22, you can see how these are used to produce an Em6/9 chord by moving to the 17th fret node. Example 23 shows the harmonics available on the open E string. Steve explores the whole concept of harmonics in *Advanced Rock Bass*.

Example 21

This solo piece by Steve is a great right hand study. The melody is played on the G and C strings while the open D pedal tone is played "In the cracks."

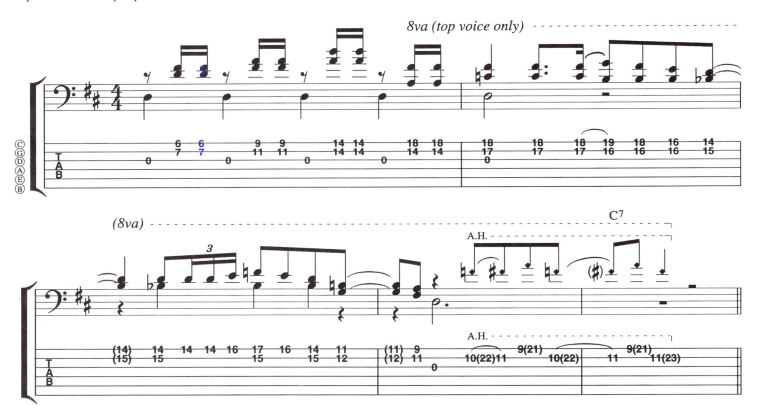

Example 22

This piece also serves as an excellent example of harmonic technique. You will notice that Steve ascends through the arpeggio using harmonics at the octave (12 frets higher than the fretted notes), he then descends through the arpeggio, up a fifth, by sliding his right hand further along the neck and playing the harmonics a fifth higher (19 frets above the fretted notes.

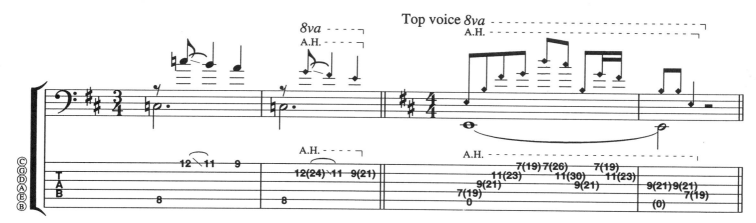

Example 23

In this example, Steve demonstrates the "E" harmonic series of artificial harmonics on the G string. Beginning with E on the 9th fret, he then plays the octave E at the 21st fret, then the 5th (B) at the 28th fret, followed by the next E at the 33rd fret and G♯ at the 37 fret. Obviously, you don't really have 37 frets on your instrument. Instead you must imagine these fret positions and locate the notes by ear. Once you find the "spot", memorize it's location. You will be surprised by how, with a little practice, you can find these "off the neck" harmonics very quickly; Steve calls this "muscle memory." Experiment, there are many other harmonics available.

Note: Harmonics follow the overtone series, which means that the same harmonics are available for all notes.

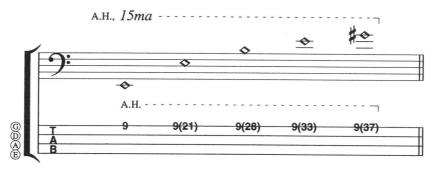

Donna Lee

This is the showpiece of this entire collection. Victor takes every concept that he has used to play funk vocabulary and uses them in the context of linear bebop lines. He uses his "double thumbing" technique (see Example 13) to play scaler lines (Example 14) and the head (Example 25). Although this seems mind-boggling, there is a pattern to it. When playing an eighth note scale passage he uses down/up strokes of the thumb. Triplets are played: thumb down – thumb up – pop. Finally arpeggios are played: thumb – hammer – index – middle. All of these techniques are demonstrated in Example 25A.

In addition to some incredible soloing, Steve does some great comping on this track (Example 26). Note how he uses artificial harmonics throughout to make the chord voicings more interesting and clear.

Example 24

In order to play *Donna Lee* with the incredible speed and driving feel with which he does, Victor uses a down-up stroke with the thumb combined with an index finger pluck (see Example 13). To gain command of this technique practice the following C major scale using the indicated right hand fingerings.

Example 25

Here is the first section of *Donna Lee* with complete right hand fingerings.

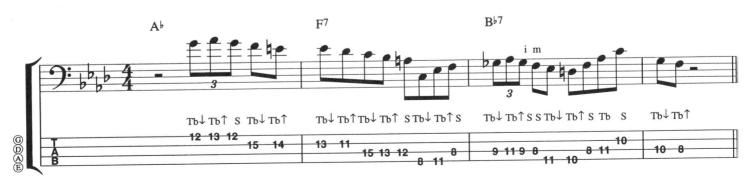

Here are the three basic techniques that Victor uses when playing the head to *Donna Lee.*

Example 25A

Example 26

While Victor plays the head, Steve comps the chord changes using voicings and comping patterns very similar to what a guitar player would use.

Chord Voicings:

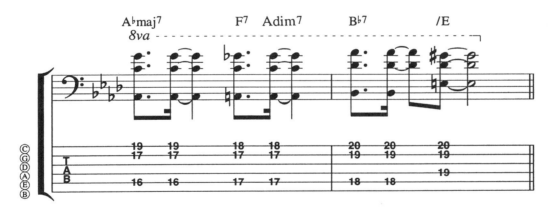

With Harmonics Added:

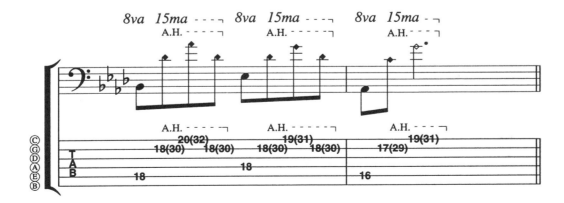

A Chick From Corea

by Steve Baily and Victor Wooten

Bangkok Blues

by Steve Bailey and Victor Wooton

Stan the Man

by Steve Bailey and Victor Wooten

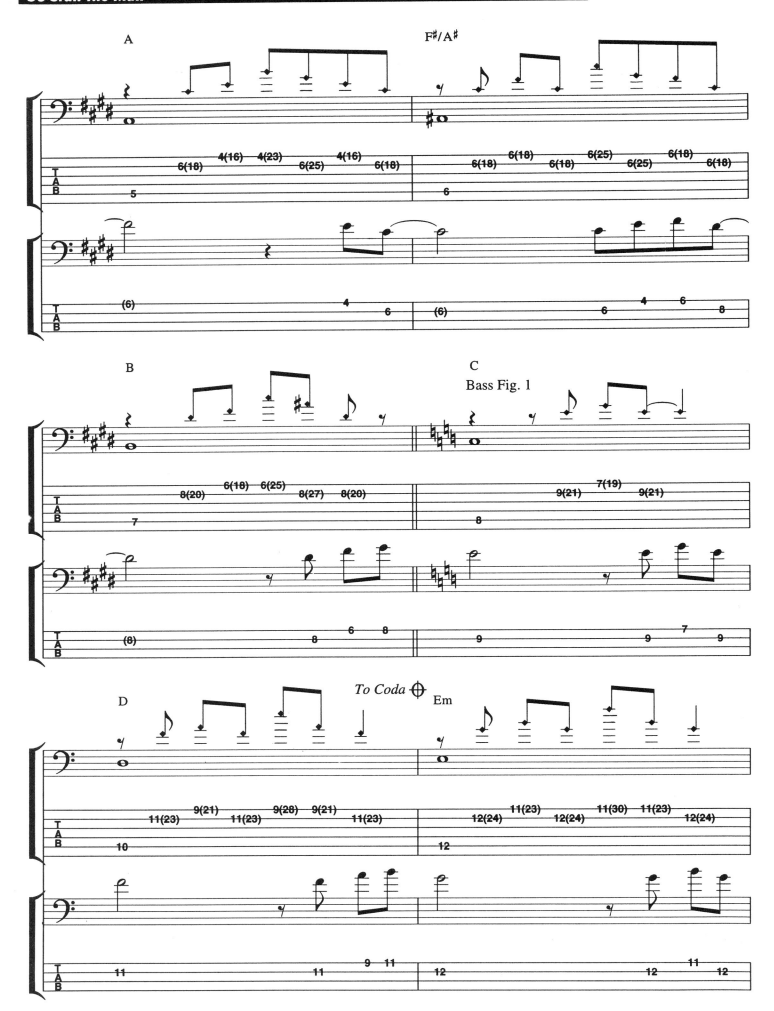

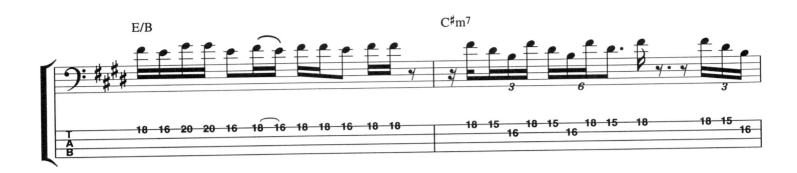

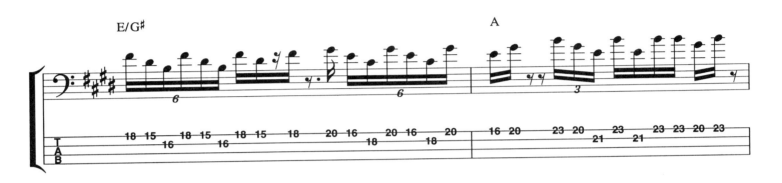

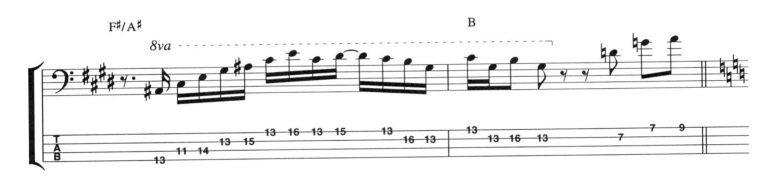

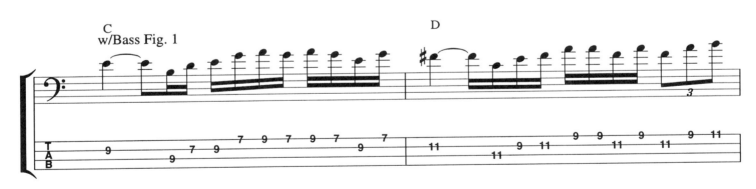

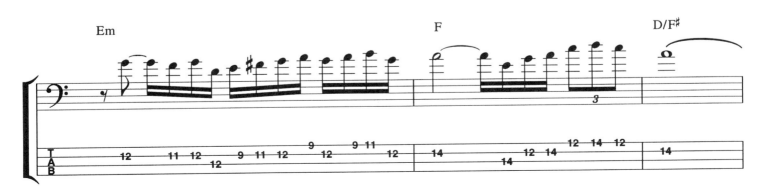

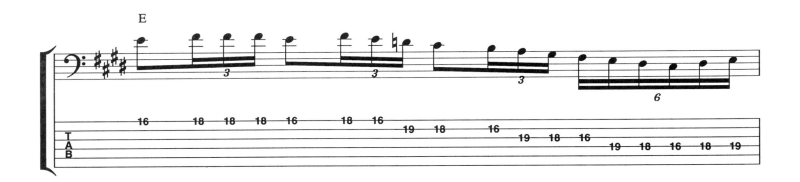

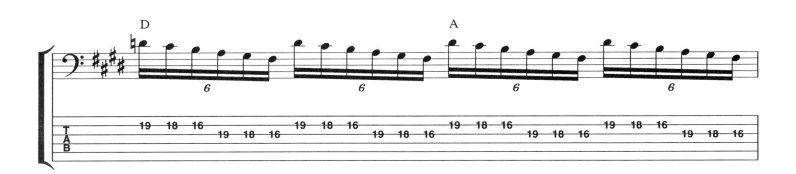

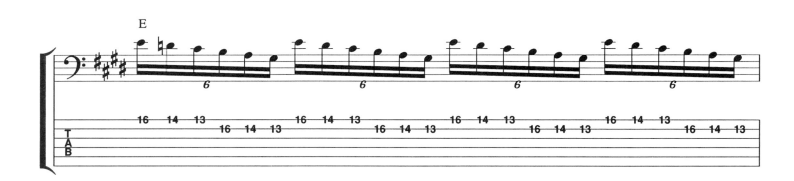

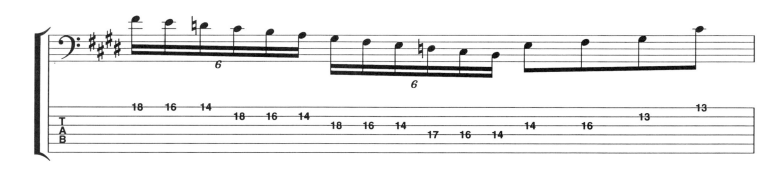

BASS

Extremes

STEVE BAILEY

VICTOR WOOTEN

Victor's Jam

by Victor Wooten

Thumb Start My Harley

by Steve Bailey and Victor Wooten

(Steve tacet)

Victor's Solo:

Emerald Forest

by Steve Bailey and Victor Wooten

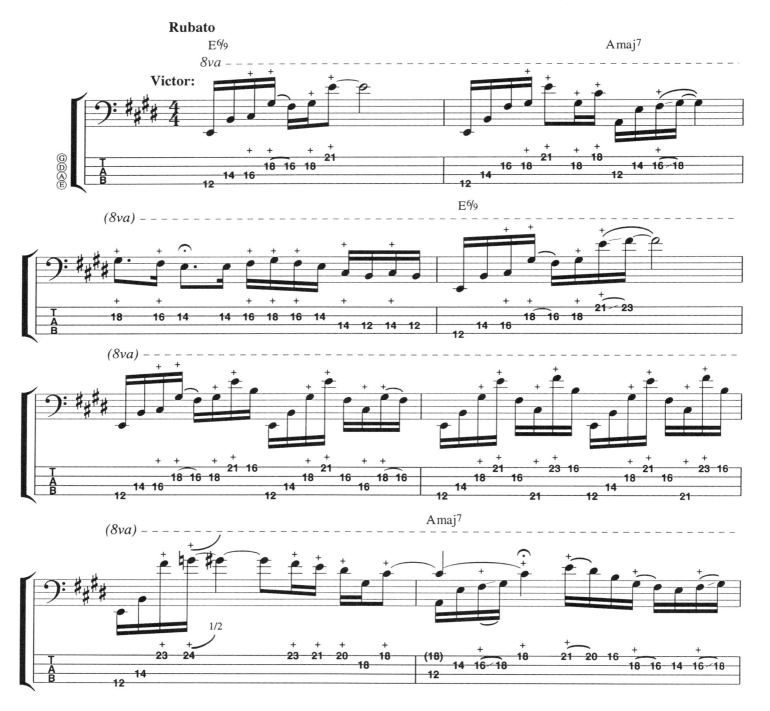

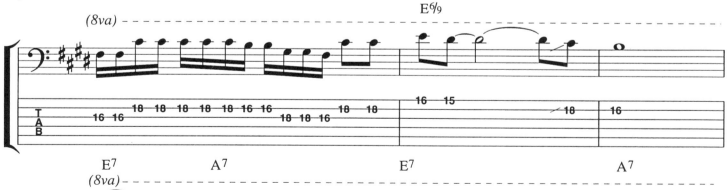

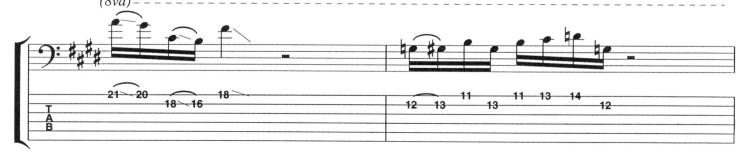

(Victor continues simile w/Bass Figs. 1 and 2)

Moonridge

by Steve Bailey

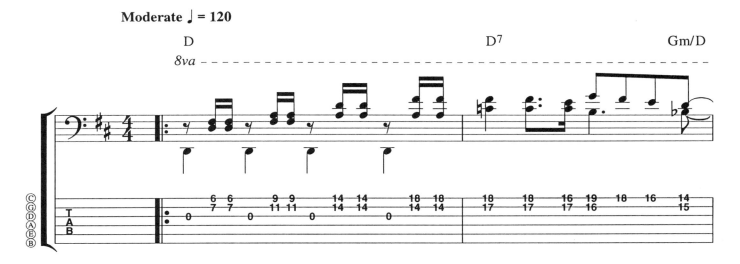

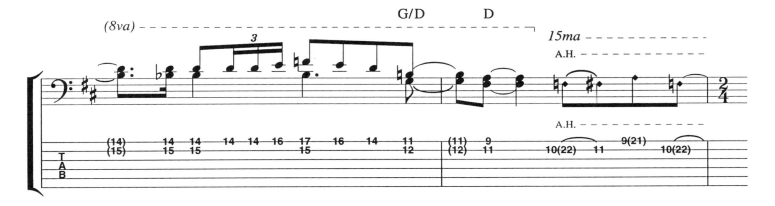

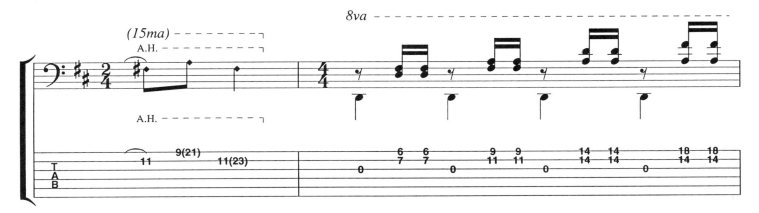

Donna Lee

by Charlie Parker

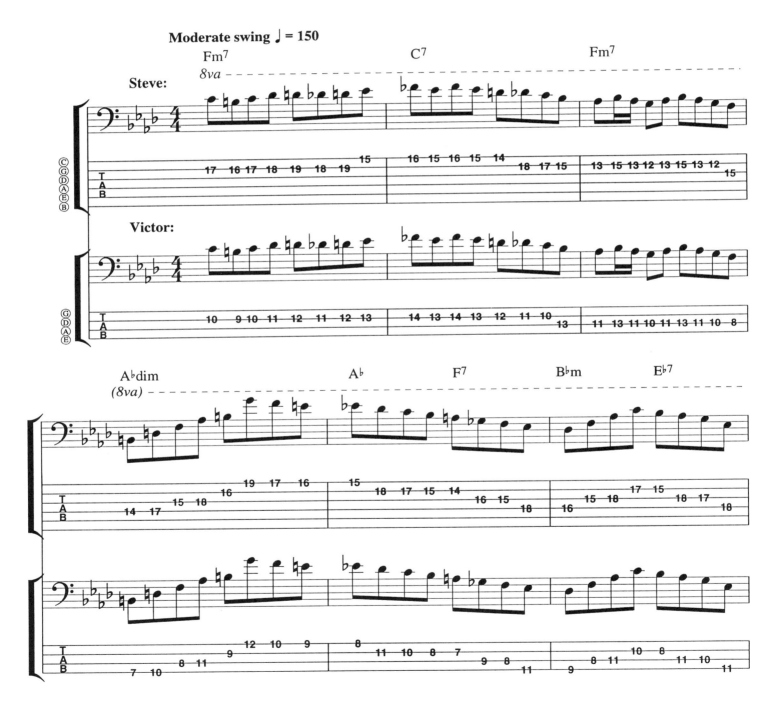

⊕ *Coda*

N.C. (Em⁷)

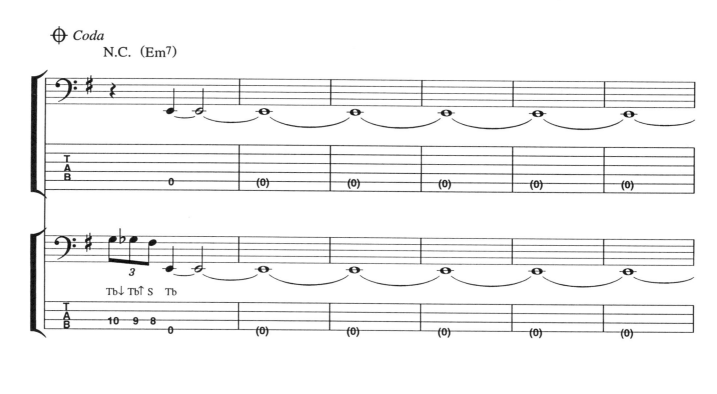

Vamp (Em)

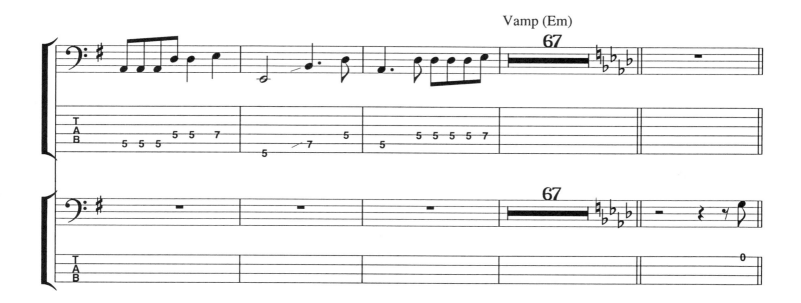

THE BEST IN VIDEO AND BOOKS

   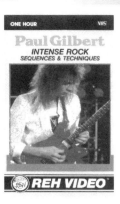  

BOOKS WITH AUDIO

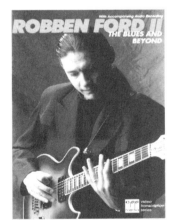   

BASS GUITAR TAB GLOSSARY

TABLATURE EXPLANATION

TABLATURE is a four line staff that graphically represents the Bass fretboard. The numbers are the frets and the lines are the strings. The low E string is on the bottom and the G string is on the top.

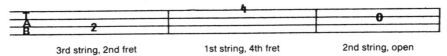

3rd string, 2nd fret   1st string, 4th fret   2nd string, open

BEND (half step): Play the note and bend up ½ step (one fret).

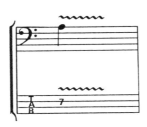

VIBRATO: The string is vibrated by shaking a held note with the fret hand. (Shake the finger, wrist, and forearm.)

SLIDE: Same as above except the second note is struck.

BEND (whole step): Play the note and bend up a whole step. (2 frets)

SLIDE: Strike the string from an unspecified pitch (usually one or two frets away) and slide into the note/fret.

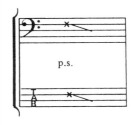

PICK SLIDE: (Nail Slide): The edge of the pick is slid down the edge of the string or string(s).

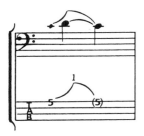

BEND and RELEASE: Play the note and gradually bend to the next pitch, then release to the original note.

SLIDE: Play the note and slide up an indefinite number of frets releasing the finger pressure near the end of the slide.

HAMMER ON: Play the lower note, then sound the higher note by hammering on with finger without picking it.

PREBEND and RELEASE: Bend the string, play it, then release to the original note.

SLIDE (Gliss): The first note is struck, then the same finger of the fret hand moves up or down the string to the location of the second note. The second note is not struck.

PULL OFF: Place both fingers on notes to be sounded. Play the higher note, then sound the lower note by pulling off the higher while keeping the lower note fretted.

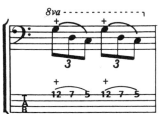

FRETBOARD TAPPING: Hammer on to the fretboard with the index or middle finger of the pick hand, then pull off to the note fretted by the fret hand.

SNAP: Usually combined with the thumb technique, one of the fingers is plucked up to create a "snap." This is done on the higher strings and can alternate with the thumb.

TRILL: The smaller notes (or numbers in parentheses) are hammered on and pulled off over and over for the length of the note.

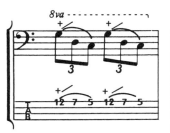

TAP SLIDE and TAP PICK SLIDE: Same as Fretboard tapping but the finger or pick taps, slides up, then is pulled off to the fretted notes.

TREMOLO: The note is struck as rapidly and continously as possible.

STACCATO (Short Notes): Notes should be played as short as possible. (Separated from one another)

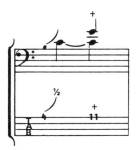

BEND AND TAP ON TECHNIQUE: Strike the note and bend up ½ or whole steps, then tap on the same string with pick hand fingertip at correct pitch or fret.

OPEN HARMONIC (Natural Harmonic): The fret hand lightly touches the string over the fret indicated; then it is struck. A chime sound is produced.

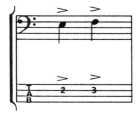

ACCENT: Note should be played with special emphasis creating an accent.

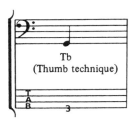

THUMB TECHNIQUE: Strike the string with the side of the outstretched thumb of the pick hand. (This is done with a wrist motion)

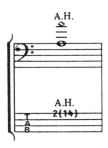

ARTIFICIAL HARMONIC: The fret hand frets the note indicated. The pick hand produces the harmonic by using a finger to lightly touch the string at the fret indicated in parentheses and plucking with another finger.

CHOPPY PHRASING: Notes should be accented with extreme staccato.

PALM MUTE: The note(s) is partially muted by the palm of the pick hand lightly touching the string(s) just before the bridge.

Steve Bailey

Steve Bailey • Bass Guitar Series

Five String Bass
____ (F3109BGX) $10.95
Five String Bass explores the fretboard in relation to the added fifth string, enabling you to fully integrate the expanded range and added possibilities of this instrument into your playing style. Beginning with position studies, the book progresses to intervals, extended scales, chord voicings, and arpeggio studies.

Fretless Bass
____ (F3108BGXAT) with Cassette $16.95
____ (F3108BGXCD) with CD $19.95
Fretless Bass is meant for the player who wishes to add this instrument to his arsenal. The book focuses on developing accurate intonation, then progresses to special effects such as harmonics, double stops, nuances idiomatic to the fretless bass, and numerous solo bass etudes.

Rock Bass
____ (F3106BGXAT) with Cassette $16.95
____ (F3106BGXCD) with CD $19.95
An aid to gaining complete technical control and understanding of the bass. Starting with right hand alternation studies, the book progresses to 3-finger technique, intervallic studies, double stops, chords, and time studies. With hazard studies and finger-busters. In standard notation and tab.

Six String Bass
____ (F3110BGX) $9.95
Six String Bass is written to help you make the transition from either the four or five string bass to the six string. The book begins with an exploration of the low B and high C strings followed by scale studies, random note studies, technique, and chord voicings (triads, seventh chords and inversions).

Advanced Rock Bass
____ (F3107BGXAT) with Cassette $16.95
____ (F3107BGXCD) with CD $19.95
Advanced Rock Bass is written for players ready for a serious challenge. Includes: string crossing exercises, double stops, odd meters, harmonics, artificial harmonics, arpeggios and chords in harmonics, thumb position, and solo bass playing. Written in standard notation and tablature.

Steve Bailey has toured and performed with Paquito D'Rivera, Dizzy Gillespie, Ira Sullivan, Larry Carlton, The Rippingtons, David Benoit, T Lavitz, Kitaro and many others. Steve is a very versatile bassist, equally at home in jazz or heavy metal situations. He is a master of all basses — four, five, and six string, fretted and fretless, electric and upright.